LET'S COOK WITH
Cereal!

Delicious & Fun Cereal Dishes Kids Can Make

Nancy Tuminelly

Consulting Editor, Diane Craig, M.A./Reading Specialist

A Division of ABDO
ABDO
Publishing Company

visit us at www.abdopublishing.com

Published by ABDO Publishing Company, a division of ABDO, P.O. Box 398166, Minneapolis, Minnesota 55439.
Copyright © 2013 by Abdo Consulting Group, Inc. International copyrights reserved in all countries. No part of this book may be reproduced in any form without written permission from the publisher. Super SandCastle™ is a trademark and logo of ABDO Publishing Company.

Printed in the United States of America, North Mankato, Minnesota
062012
092012

♻ PRINTED ON RECYCLED PAPER

Editor: Liz Salzmann
Content Developer: Nancy Tuminelly
Cover and Interior Design and Production: Colleen Dolphin, Mighty Media, Inc.
Food Production: Desirée Bussiere
Photo Credits: Colleen Dolphin, Shutterstock, iStockphoto (Gary Milner, Dawna Stafford, Mark Swallow)

The following manufacturers/names appearing in this book are trademarks: Breyers® Ice Cream, Gold Medal® All-Purpose Flour, Kraft® Jet-Puffed Marshmallow Creme, Market Pantry® Pure Vanilla Extract, McCormick® Imitation Almond Extract, Morton's® Iodized Salt, Proctor Silex® Hand Blender, Pyrex® Measuring Glass, Roundy's® Cream Cheese

Library of Congress Cataloging-in-Publication Data
Tuminelly, Nancy, 1952-
  Let's cook with cereal! : delicious & fun cereal dishes kids can make / Nancy Tuminelly.
    p. cm. -- (Super simple recipes)
  ISBN 978-1-61783-419-6
  1. Cooking (Cereals)--Juvenile literature. 2. Snack foods--Juvenile literature. I. Title.
  TX808.T86 2013
  641.6'31--dc23
                              2011052135

Super SandCastle™ books are created by a team of professional educators, reading specialists, and content developers around five essential components—phonemic awareness, phonics, vocabulary, text comprehension, and fluency—to assist young readers as they develop reading skills and strategies and increase their general knowledge. All books are written, reviewed, and leveled for guided reading, early reading intervention, and Accelerated Reader® programs for use in shared, guided, and independent reading and writing activities to support a balanced approach to literacy instruction.

Note to Adult Helpers

Helping kids learn how to cook is fun! It's a great way to practice math and science. Cooking teaches kids about responsibility and boosts their confidence. Plus, they learn how to help out in the kitchen! The recipes in this book require adult assistance. Make sure there is always an adult around when kids are in the kitchen. Expect kids to make a mess, but also expect them to clean up after themselves. Most importantly, make the experience pleasurable by sharing and enjoying the food kids make.

Symbols

Knife
Always ask an adult to help you use knives.

Microwave
Be careful with hot food! Learn more on page 7.

Oven
Have an adult help put things into and take them out of the oven. Learn more on page 7.

Stovetop
Be careful around hot burners! Learn more on page 7.

Nuts
Some people can get very sick if they eat nuts.

Contents

Let's Cook with Cereal!

Cereal is the most popular breakfast food in America! It is also a great snack anytime. Cereal is fast, easy, and good for you.

Cereal is made from grain. Cereal can be hot or cold. The oldest known cereal was grain cooked in water or milk. It was called porridge or gruel.

Cold cereal became popular in the 1860s. People wanted breakfast food that was faster to make. But they wanted it to be healthy too. Cold cereal has fiber and **protein**. It also has added **vitamins**. Some cereals have too much added sugar.

The recipes in this book are simple. It's fun using one main ingredient! Cooking teaches you about food, measuring, and following directions. Enjoy your tasty treats with your family and friends!

Think Safety!

- Ask an adult to help you use knives. Use a cutting board.

- Clean up spills to prevent accidents.

- Keep tools and **utensils** away from the edge of the table or counter.

- Use a step stool if you cannot reach something.

- Tie back long hair or wear a hat.

- Don't wear loose clothes. Roll up long **sleeves**.

- Keep a fire extinguisher in the cooking area.

Cooking Basics

Before you start...

- Get **permission** from an adult.

- Wash your hands.

- Read the recipe at least once.

- Set out all the ingredients and tools you will need.

When you're done...

- Cover food with plastic wrap or aluminum foil. Use **containers** with lids if you have them.

- Wash all of the dishes and **utensils**.

- Put all of the ingredients and tools back where you found them.

- Clean up your work space.

Using the Microwave

- Use microwave-safe dishes.

- Never put aluminum foil or metal in the microwave.

- Start with a short cook time. If it's not enough, cook it some more.

- Use oven mitts when taking things out of the microwave.

- Stop the microwave to stir liquids during heating.

Using the Stovetop

- Turn pot handles away from the burners and the edge of the stove.

- Use the temperature setting in the recipe.

- Use pot holders to handle hot pots and pans.

- Do not leave metal **utensils** in pots.

- Don't put anything except pots and pans on or near the burners.

- Use a timer. Check the food and cook it more if needed.

Using the Oven

- Use the temperature setting in the recipe.

- Preheat the oven while making the recipe.

- Use oven-safe dishes.

- Use pot holders or oven mitts to handle baking sheets and dishes.

- Do not touch oven doors. They can be very hot.

- Set a timer. Check the food and bake it more if needed.

A microwave, stovetop, and oven are very useful for cooking food. But they can be **dangerous** if you are not careful. Always ask an adult for help.

Measuring

Wet Ingredients

Set a measuring cup on the counter. Add the liquid until it reaches the amount you need. Check the measurement from eye level.

Dry Ingredients

Use a spoon to put the dry ingredient in the measuring cup or spoon. Put more than you need in the measuring cup or spoon. Run the back of a dinner knife across the top. This removes the extra.

Moist Ingredients

Moist ingredients are things such as brown sugar and dried fruit. They need to be packed down into the measuring cup. Keep packing until the ingredient reaches the measurement line.

Do You Know This = That?

There are different ways to measure the same amount.

 = | |||| = | ||||| + | = |

3 teaspoons   1 tablespoon   4 tablespoons   ¼ cup   5 tablespoons   1 teaspoon   ⅓ cup

16 tablespoons   1 cup   1 cup   8 ounces   1 stick of butter   ½ cup

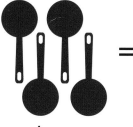 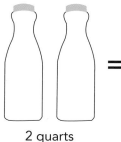 

2 cups   1 pint   4 cups   1 quart   2 quarts   ½ gallon

Cooking Terms

Grease
Coat a dish or baking sheet with butter or oil.

Whisk
Stir quickly by hand with a whisk or fork.

Slice
Cut something into thin pieces with a knife.

Spread
Make a smooth layer with a spoon, knife, or spatula.

Grate
Shred something into small pieces using a grater.

Chill
Put something in the refrigerator for a while.

Beat
Stir something with a mixer until it is smooth.

Cube
Cut something into small squares.

What's Good for You?

Most cereals are in one of four main groups. They are whole grain, bran, organic, and sugary cereals.

Whole Grain Cereal

Cereal grains include wheat, corn, oats, rice, and barley. Whole grain cereals are made from one or more types of grain. They are at least 25% oat or bran. They have little or no added sugars.

Bran Cereal

Bran is the outside covering of oats, wheat, or rice whole grains. It has a lot of fiber. Bran cereals make you feel full for a long time.

Organic Cereal

Organic cereals are made from grains grown without chemicals. They also don't have added **vitamins** and **minerals**.

Sugary Cereal

Sugary cereals are the least healthy for you. Many of the **nutrients** have been taken out of the grains. They have a lot of added sugar and **preservatives**. Try not to eat sugary cereal very often.

Tools

sharp knife

9 × 13-inch
baking sheet

dinner knife

mixing spoon

cutting board

rolling pin

timer

liquid measuring cup

oven mitts

hand mixer

wax paper

small bowls

dry measuring cups

measuring spoons

large microwave-safe
bowl

rubber spatula

large plastic
zipper bags

plastic wrap

large pot

pot holders

tall glasses

cookie cutters

container with lid

spoon

whisk

ice cream scoop

mixing bowls

9 × 9-inch
baking dish

9 × 13-inch
baking dish

Ingredients

cream cheese

strawberry yogurt

honey

eggs

salt

sharp cheddar cheese

peanut butter

bananas

butter

strawberries

miniature marshmallows

sprinkles

lemon juice

ice cream

all-purpose flour

sweetened condensed milk

sesame seeds

miniature
chocolate chips

marshmallow
creme

raisins

sugar

ground cinnamon

toasted oat cereal

crispy rice cereal

vanilla extract

corn flake cereal

whole grain
wheat flake cereal

chocolate puffed
cereal

almond extract

flaked coconut

quick-cooking oats

granola

15

Corn Flake Balls

A healthy snack that's good any time!

Makes 8 balls

ingredients

1 cup peanut butter
½ cup honey
3½ cups corn flake cereal
sesame seeds

tools

large microwave-safe bowl
pot holders
measuring cups
mixing spoon
small bowl
timer

1. Mix peanut butter and honey in a large, microwave-safe bowl. Microwave on high for 1 minute. Stir well.

2. Add the cereal to the peanut butter mixture. Stir well. Chill the mixture for 30 minutes.

3. Divide the mixture into eight pieces. Roll them into balls.

4. Put the sesame seeds in a small bowl. Roll the balls in the seeds until they are covered. Chill them until they are hard.

Sunrise Surprise

A tasty way to start your day!

Makes 12 bars

ingredients

1 stick butter

1 teaspoon vanilla extract

½ cup peanut butter

2 7-ounce jars
   marshmallow crème

1 cup whole grain
   wheat flake cereal

1 cup granola

tools

large microwave-safe bowl

measuring spoons

pot holders

mixing spoon

measuring cups

hand mixer

9 × 13-inch baking dish

rubber spatula

plastic wrap

1 Put butter and vanilla in a large microwave-safe bowl. Microwave on high for 1 minute. The butter should be melted. Mix well with a spoon.

2 Add the peanut butter and marshmallow to the butter mixture. Beat with a mixer.

3 Add the cereal. Mix well. Pour the mixture into the baking dish. Spread it evenly.

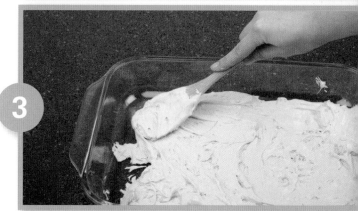

4 Sprinkle the granola evenly over the cereal. Press it lightly with a rubber spatula.

5 Cover the dish with plastic wrap. Chill for one hour. Cut it into 12 squares.

Crispy Cheese Puffies

Perfect for lunch or an after-school snack!

Makes 48 puffs

ingredients

2 cups all-purpose flour
1 cup butter
2 cups sharp cheddar, grated
4 cups crispy rice cereal

tools

measuring cups
large mixing bowl
hand mixer
mixing spoon
9 × 13-inch baking sheet
oven mitts
container with lid

1 Preheat the oven to 400 **degrees**. Put the flour, butter, and cheese in a large mixing bowl. Beat with a mixer.

2 Stir in the cereal. **Squeeze** the mixture with your hands until it is thick and well mixed.

3 Pinch off small pieces. Roll them into balls. Put them on the baking sheet.

4 Bake for 10 to 15 minutes. They should turn golden.

5 Cool for 30 minutes. Store them in a **container** in the refrigerator.

Scrumptious Squares

A gooey, chocolatey, sweet treat!

Makes 48 bars

ingredients

9 cups crispy rice cereal

6½ cups quick-cooking oats

1 cup corn flake cereal

1 cup flaked coconut

26½ ounces miniature
marshmallows

1 cup butter, cubed

½ cup honey

½ cup raisins

1 cup miniature
chocolate chips

tools

large mixing
bowl

measuring
cups

large
microwave-
safe bowl

mixing spoon

pot holders

2 9 × 13-inch
baking dishes,
greased

dinner knife

1   Mix the crispy rice cereal, oats, corn flake cereal, and coconut in a large bowl.

2   Put the marshmallows and butter in a large microwave-safe bowl. Microwave on high for 1 to 2 minutes. Stir until smooth. Stir in the honey.

3   Pour the marshmallow mixture over the cereal mixture. Mix until the cereal is coated. Cool for 5 minutes.

4   Mix in raisins and miniature chocolate chips.

5   Press half of the mixture into each baking dish.

6   Cool for 30 minutes. Cut into squares and enjoy!

Flaky Coconut Kisses

These are so delicious you can't stop eating them!

Makes 12 cookies

ingredients

3 egg whites

½ teaspoon salt

1½ cups sugar

½ teaspoon almond extract

1 cup flaked coconut

3 cups whole grain
    wheat flake cereal

tools

large mixing bowl

measuring spoons

whisk

measuring cups

mixing spoon

9 × 13-inch baking sheet,
    greased

oven mitts

timer

1 Preheat the oven to 325 **degrees**. Put the egg whites and salt in a large mixing bowl. Whisk well. Gradually whisk the sugar into the egg white mixture.

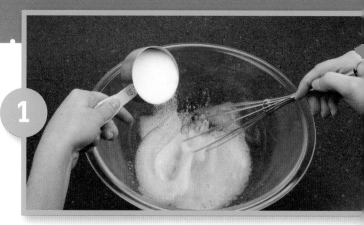

2 Mix in the almond extract. Mix in the coconut and cereal. Stir well.

3 Drop tablespoons of the mixture onto the baking sheet. Bake for 15 to 25 minutes. Remove them from the baking sheet right away.

TIP: To separate an egg, crack it in the middle. Hold it over a bowl. Pull the eggshell apart. Gently pass the egg back and forth between the halves of the shell. The egg white will fall into the bowl. The yolk will stay in the shell.

Ice Cream Snack-wich

Enjoy these crunchy, creamy treats on a hot day!

Makes 12 snacks

ingredients

3 tablespoons butter
4 cups miniature
    marshmallows
2 teaspoons vanilla extract
6 cups crispy rice cereal
sprinkles
2 pints ice cream

tools

measuring cups
large pot
mixing spoon
measuring spoons
9 × 13-inch baking sheet,
    greased
wax paper
cookie cutters, greased
ice cream scoop
timer

1   Melt the butter in a large pot over low heat. Add the marshmallows. Stir until they are melted.

2   Remove from heat. Stir in the vanilla. Add the crispy rice cereal. Stir until the cereal is coated.

3   Put the mixture on the baking sheet. Use a piece of wax paper to press the mixture evenly. Add sprinkles on top. Press them down. Chill for 15 minutes.

4   Press a cookie cutter into the cereal mixture. Cut out 24 cereal cookies.

5   Put a scoop of ice cream on 12 of the cookies. Put the other cookies on top to make **sandwiches**. Freeze them for 30 minutes before serving.

Cocoa & Fruit Parfait

A breakfast treat that's sweet, smooth, and crunchy!

Makes 2 servings

ingredients

18 ounces strawberry yogurt
2 cups chocolate puffed cereal
2 bananas, sliced
2 strawberries

tools

2 tall glasses
measuring cups
spoon
sharp knife
cutting board

1 Put ⅓ cup yogurt in each glass. Add ¼ cup cereal. Add a layer of banana slices.

 2 Add 2 spoonfuls of yogurt, ¼ cup cereal, and a layer of banana slices. Repeat until the glasses are almost full.

 3 Top each **parfait** with a strawberry. Your parfaits are ready to serve!

TIP: Try adding other fruit to the mix! Blueberries, raspberries, and orange slices are all fun ingredients.

Lemon Delight Bars

A sweet, tart, and creamy cereal treat!

Makes 9 bars

ingredients

3 cups toasted oat cereal

⅓ cup butter, melted

1 teaspoon ground cinnamon

1 tablespoon sugar

8 ounces cream cheese, softened

14-ounce can sweetened condensed milk

¼ cup lemon juice

1 teaspoon vanilla extract

tools

measuring cups

measuring spoons

large plastic zipper bag

rolling pin

mixing bowls

mixing spoon

small bowl

9 × 9-inch baking dish

oven mitts

hand mixer

1. Preheat the oven to 375 **degrees**. Zip the cereal inside the plastic bag. Roll over it with a rolling pin to crush the cereal.

2. Stir the butter, cinnamon, and sugar together in a large bowl. Mix in the cereal **crumbs**. Set aside 2 tablespoons of the mixture.

3. Press the rest of the cereal mixture into the baking dish. Bake for 9 minutes. This is the crust.

4. Beat the cream cheese with a hand mixer. Slowly add the condensed milk. Stir in the lemon juice and vanilla. Spread the cream cheese mixture over the crust.

5. Sprinkle the cereal mixture you set aside on top. Chill for one hour.

Glossary

container – something that other things can be put into.

crumb – a tiny piece of something, especially something baked, such as bread or crackers.

dangerous – able or likely to cause harm or injury.

degree – the unit used to measure temperature.

mineral – a natural element that plants, animals, and people need to be healthy.

nutrient – something that helps living things grow. Vitamins, minerals, and proteins are nutrients.

parfait – a dessert made with layers of fruit and either ice cream or yogurt.

permission – when a person in charge says it's okay to do something.

preservative – a chemical added to food to keep it from spoiling or changing color.

protein – a substance needed for good health, found naturally in meat, eggs, beans, nuts, and milk.

sandwich – two pieces of something flat, such as bread, with a filling in the middle.

sleeve – the part of a piece of clothing that covers some or all of the arm.

squeeze – to press or grip something tightly.

utensil – a tool used to prepare or eat food.

vitamin – a substance needed for good health, found naturally in plants and meats.